I have a kind of fear

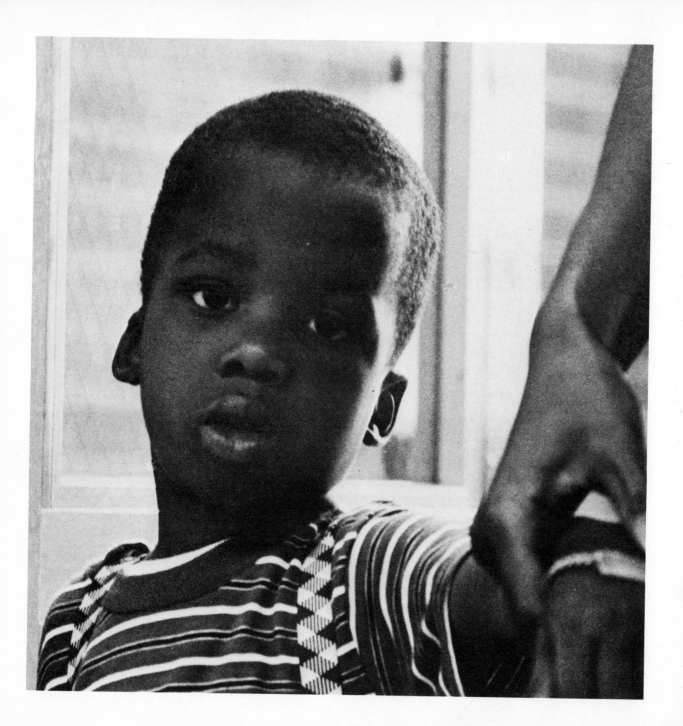

I have done so little
For you,
And you have done so little
For me,
That we have good reason
Never to agree.

I, however,
Have such meagre
Power
Clutching at a
Moment,
While you control
An hour.

But your hour is
A stone.

My moment is
A flower.

—Langston Hughes,
Poet to Bigot

Confessions from the writings of white teachers and black students in city schools. Edited by Richard Larson and James Olson. Photographs by Howard M. Berliant. Quadrangle Books. Chicago.

I have a kind of fear

The problems of inner-city schools have been so thoroughly described that words like alienation, relevance, culture-clash, and deprivation have become popular clichés.

Black militants seek control of schools in some cities, and superintendents become harder and harder to find. Whites who feared integration now fear segregation. Black power is a concept that bewilders them. New teachers avoid the cities in increasing numbers. The school-achievement gap that separates the children of the urban poor from those of the middle-class suburbs is as wide as ever. Communication between groups has all but ended.

This book looks at inner-city schools from within, with the hope that its readers will gain some insights into the complexities of urban education. Its content is comprised of vignettes, conversations, descriptions, poems, questions, and other entries taken from journals kept by urban teachers who recorded their daily impressions of schools and the people in them. The writings neither preach nor lecture. There are no theories clarified, no teaching methods elaborated. The book is not an exposé, nor is it a how-to-do-it primer. It is, simply, descriptive. The reader may draw his own conclusions about the social issues mirrored in daily schoolroom incidents; he may apply his own values and feelings to this microcosm of America's social dynamite.

"I have a kind of fear," writes one author, about to take her first teaching assignment. Her fear is grounded in the white American dilemma: trapped in a heritage of racism, she is apprehensive about the unknown black people she will inevitably confront. In the honest recognition of her fear there is an expression of hope, a hope that characterizes many of the writings in this book.

There is hope, for example, in the kind of teaching the writers seem to value. An interaction with children that is open and caring supersedes adherence to lists of rules made by the insecure establishment. Concern for relevant learning overrides the need to follow the book. Enthusiasm about teaching is high, and the writers have a pervasive sense of anger and frustration about the injustices wrought on children by mechanical, rigid institutions and by stony schoolmen.

There is optimism in the teachers' observations about the impact of their attitudes on inner-city children. The writers have recorded in their journals a profound despair over bigotry and stereotypical thinking among teachers. They have known the inevitable, hostile response by pupils. They have seen teachers react to hostility. Their writing suggests that good teaching can reduce that conflict. See your students as human beings. Have a sense of humor. Expect a lot. Examine yourself, root out old biases, and become believable to your students. Build new understanding from mistakes, whether you or your students make them. Care enough to extend teaching beyond the classroom. Value differences more than sameness, controversy more than consensus, and communication more than silence. You are neither a policeman, nor a clerk, nor a keeper of the grounds. You are a teacher.

Hope lies also in the teachers' strong dissatisfaction with their professional preparation. They have not gone to work prepared. The suburban model of teacher training doesn't fit, and the teacher across the hall is of little help.

While the tone of the book is optimistic, some of the entries are not. The reader will encounter expressions of hopelessness and despair. He will confront the incredible damage done to children through systematic, institutionalized processes. He will see why teachers quit. But that serves only as counterpoint to the reasons why they stay: they are good at their work, they are needed, and their accomplishments are rewarding. We hope that teachers, students, and others may spend an evening with this book—and end it asking new questions.

We are indebted to Mrs. Julia Roth and Mr. Antoine Lintereur for their contributions to this book. Their observations as teachers were used frequently and added a great measure of sensitivity that would otherwise not have been present.

Contributors

Howard Berliant
Mary Bushel
Georgia Casper
Donald Darnieder
Barbara Ellis
Nancy Fall
John Glaris
Alice Gruenberg
Gerald Hauser
Gayle Irwin
Judy Kirkhorn
Richard Larson
Norma Letourneau
Sarah Lewis
Antoine Lintereur
Shirley Littlejohn
Greg Millman
James Olson
Lynn Patner
Noelia Pessoa
Julia Roth
H. Henry Whang
Gurney Williams
Patricia Wiser
Lauri Wynn
Lynn Zimmerman

I have a kind of fear

I have a kind of fear . . .

I have come to realize what an important part my
background has played in influencing my views
toward the Negro.

Although I have moved into an area where Negro
families live near, I have not gotten to know any
yet. I have a kind of fear. I am not able to look at a
Negro without seeing his color first. There are a few
classmates here at the university who are Negro.
Getting to know them and talk to them has helped
me a lot.

But in my home they are always referred to as
niggers, and the area they live in is the slum or the
black forest. When there is a civil rights
demonstration or something more violent, such as a
riot, one member of my family might say, "They
ought to slaughter all of them."

I don't want to blame my environment for my
outlook, but I am aware that there is something
there that I have to learn to overcome.

Some subliminal second thoughts

He's in my classroom, but he didn't choose to be
    there . . .
He didn't choose this school, and he didn't choose
    me as his teacher.
He didn't select his father's income, his mother's
    absence, or his crowded house.
He didn't choose to confound my pat curriculum
    and my pet teaching prescriptions.
He didn't choose to value different things than I, or
    to speak in a different, albeit more colorful, idiom;
He just didn't choose . . .
He can't smile nicely when his world tells him to feel
    anger, nor can he frown away warmth and fair
    play . . . his mask is not like mine.
He could never comprehend the gap that separates
    his mercurial moods from my pale, practiced
    rightness.
He didn't decide one day to shape his nose, his
    brow, or his mouth into forms that trigger my
    discomfort and disdain.
He doesn't know that he won't learn if I don't think
    he can, or that my eyes and voice limit his circle of
    friends.
He doesn't know how much his future depends
    on me.
He just doesn't know . . .

"For tomorrow, write a theme on pride"

My mother was a bad girl in Chicago. My fader find
her on state street with bad men, she was fiting
them. My fader took her home with hem and washed
her up and take her to church. She desided to be a
good girl. They moved to Racine. Then I was borned.
I growed up hear and have a better life than my
mother have in Chicago. When I bring a boy home
with me, I can ask him to stay for super, he is
wellcom. My father talk to them and make them feel
rite at home. My mother keep the house meat and
clearn all time, and she manage my fathers pay
check real good. At the super tabel when my friend
is eaten, my father says have anuther bork shop. I am
proud of my parent. My father is color, my mother
is a white women. I am proud that he found her and
make her good. They are good parent.

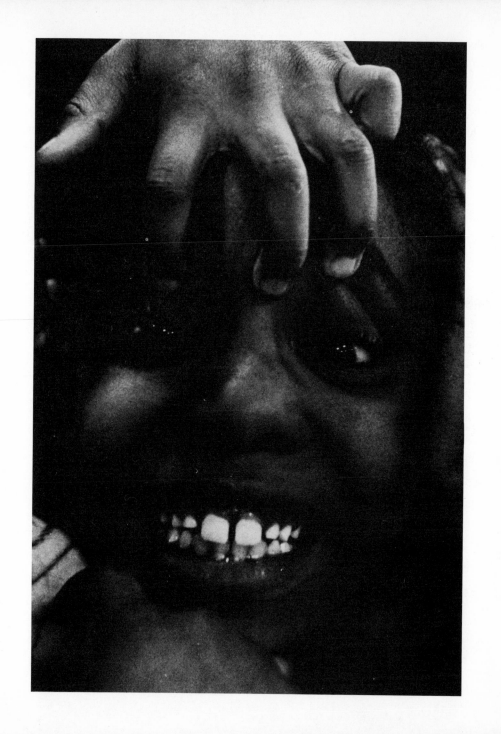

Vocational training

Afternoon at a sheltered workshop. Boys who go there are referred by the schools primarily because they're disturbed and can't fit into the academic situation. I was depressed by the dingy rooms and rows of packing boxes which are filled by these disturbed boys as their vocational training.

There oughta be a law

Why can't kids talk? The children can't talk in the hall because that is a rule. Let's go to a classroom and lissen to a teacher. Now hear, there is no talking in the halls. anyone who talks will go back to the room.

If you talk you will not have your recess. But when the teacher's see each other in the hall, you don't know who is the worst. I think why shood teacher's be able to talk and the children not be able to talk. Teacher's like children, shood not be able to talk.   *Henry*

The voice of experience—overheard

"But, I tell you, Lois, it just doesn't work. I've worked with them in Chicago, too. They just don't respond to reason. You have to use force. You have to be forceful with them. In Chicago, too. I learned that in Chicago. If you reason with them, they walk all over you. They're used to force. Use force. Force is the only way. Be forceful. Force . . .

Beginner's text—P₁

He hit me.
She said a bad word.
Where's my bubble gum?
Here's a Cadillac.
It is a red car.
Me first!
Give me!
I don't want it!
Get out!
Look out!
I got new shoes.
Teacher!
Teacher!
Teacher!
Teacher!
Mother
Baby
Bed
Television
Coca-Cola
Kool-Aid
Corn Flakes

Write a letter to your best friend

"Write a letter to your best friend" was an assignment today for the upper primary class—3rd grade.

The teacher showed the class a sample letter and discussed it very briefly. I wasn't sure whether the class understood it or not, but that was not my concern as an observer. She said, "You must write a letter to someone who lives outside of the city." She emphasized again that each child must write a letter to someone who lives out of the city. Naturally, children wondered and began to ask questions. Again more questions came, then she shouted to the class that everyone must think of someone, and if anyone couldn't he should stay home rather than come to school. My eyes and ears were wide open. I looked at the class. There was silence.

Head Start incident

The children were all sitting around the teacher, and she was asking them questions that would lead to more than a one-word response. One of the "charmers" got up and showed the teacher a piece of candy he had in his pocket—the candy was totally irrelevant to the discussion at hand. She asked Kevin if she could have his candy for a minute. He surrendered it, and was now sharing the center of attention with his piece of candy. With her fingers the teacher crushed the cellophane to get an appropriate crackle noise. Then she asked them what they heard. Next she held it up and asked whether they thought it was hard or soft candy. It was hard. "What color is it?" "What flavor?" (Perhaps she used taste, I'm not sure) "Strawberry—cherry—etc." Then she asked Kevin if it would be all right if she opened the paper just a bit—so they could smell it. "Sure"—when Kevin sat down after the teacher had given him back his candy, he didn't want to eat it as was his intention before, not this treasure.

The vice-principal told him to leave

A further meaningless use of rules was enforced today. I had one of my children from last semester come and visit me before school—and the vice-principal told him to leave. Why? Because if he came in early to see a teacher, then anyone could, and there would be bedlam in the school. How ridiculous and sad!

Within the school day there is really so little chance to develop one-to-one interpersonal relationships, and so I have always encouraged my children to come in before school or stay after just to talk and have some fun.

I can get around this rule by giving special-help slips to students I would like to see in the morning, but this is not the point. This is a school rule made by the teachers who want to see the children only between nine and three-fifteen. Teaching then becomes a job to be done rather than a privilege and a delight.

Jeramy

Jeramy has had a long, colorful history at our school. Last semester, when his teacher asked the students to bring feathers to class, Jeramy went out during the lunch period, killed a large pigeon, and brought the body to class. Today he was speaking to that same teacher about his current teacher, yours truly. "I have a rotten teacher this semester. He sings around his classroom so much that he even has me liking music!"

Bluebirds

It was on her first visit to her towheaded son's first grade classroom when she saw him perform in his reading group—the bluebirds—ten black children and her Timothy. She had come to witness for herself the new spurt of progress that Tim was enjoying that the teacher had so enthusiastically reported to her. She couldn't look at the progress— she blurted to the teacher, "He doesn't belong in that group," and hastily departed.

Within a month Timothy's family sold their house and moved to the suburbs where Tim was enrolled in a small school, still more rural than suburban, and placed with a strong-willed, vocal teacher who ran a tight ship and frightened the principal. Timothy can't keep up, she reported, and he was moved to kindergarten the next day.

Mother moved with dispatch. She called the school from which she'd rescued Timothy by selling her home, and re-enrolled him in his old first grade, where he rejoined the bluebirds. She didn't complain about the weekly tuition she had to pay.

You know—a conifer!

The poor child has usually had a different set of experiences. For example, Jack, a boy in the second grade in summer school, was reading to me one day from a book about our five senses. He did not know all of the words, so he frequently guessed by looking at the pictures. Thus he could sometimes come close to the intended word. One section, that about smell, was most indicative of my point here. Since he could not read "pine trees" in a sentence about their odor, I asked him if he knew what a pine tree was. He didn't. (I heard another teacher interject at this point in a similar conversation, "You know— a conifer!") Even after I described the needles, told him they are green all year, asked him about Christmas trees, and tried to describe their odor, there was no identification.

On the next page, mention was made of the smell of cookies, "fresh from the oven." Jack read it as "fresh from the *box*." Upon questioning him I discovered he was not aware that cookies ever came from an oven.

Gray stuff

The topic of discussion was different kinds of sausage. The children were talking about an older brother who was working at the sausage plant.

As the conversation progressed, they started to talk about the different kinds of sausage they liked.

I guess I imagined that since about one-third of my class was Polish, they would know quite a bit about sausage. But I shouldn't have been shocked when they talked about "this gray stuff," and "the other stuff with the spots in it." Then all of a sudden it occurred to me what they were talking about. The gray sausage was of course liver sausage, and the spotted variety was summer sausage. When I asked if they had ever used these names, the answer was no.

That cat, Brutus

Willie passed his exam on *Caesar*!!! He got excited about "that cat, Brutus," and got a 75 on the exam. He was very pleased with himself, and his delight made the day great after all.

S.A. why I have to stay after

I have to stay because teacher told me to say I am
sorry what I did, teacher. I was not talking, teacher.
I will not talk in the library. I am very sorry, teacher.
I will not talk any more. I am very sorry. I love my
teacher. I am sorry.   *LeRoy*

Today was a good day

Today was a good day. When the children came in
this morning, one asked, "Teacher, why is the flag
out in front?" The school was being used as a polling
place for the local election. I proceeded to discuss
"election" and "vote," both completely strange to
them. Then we went down to look at the precinct
polling place. Luck again—no one was there, and we
were invited in, the children were shown the
machines and how they worked, and a woman came
in to vote, so they could see it in operation. They
were given sample ballots, and when we got
upstairs I explained how one votes, and they all
voted—and they voted for only one candidate for
each office!

This certainly had more meaning than any book or
teacher lecture. They were reluctant to go home at
noon.

I know how it is

Dear Mr. Linter,

I am very sorry that I ran out on you and I know you don't like that because I play school at home and I know how it is.   *Wanda Mae*

Bedtime

"Boys and girls, how many in the class went to bed last night before 10:00 p.m.?"

(Twenty-three hands up out of twenty-seven students.)

"And how many boys and girls watched Johnny Carson last night? Please raise your hand."

(Fifteen out of twenty-seven.)

They are MY class now

I was out two days and found that really I had been sorely missed. What a pleasure to know one is needed! I have felt terribly frustrated this semester. Two days before the semester ended the principal asked me to take a higher grade than I had been teaching—filled with "difficult" kids. He flattered me, so I accepted. (My fault, not his.) So I really have started from scratch with these kids—a lot of experimentation has gone on and little has proved to be fruitful.

But what I discovered by being absent was that basically the kids are better off with me there. One serious accident occurred (a boy was choked by another to the point of hemorrhaging), and there were three other suspensions for various misdemeanors—there was a sigh of relief on the part of the whole class when I walked into the room.

They are *my* class now. We've learned to work together, play together, take care of each other to the point that these incidents would never have occurred if I had been there. Not because of an iron fist, but because *we're* a group that gets along. I only wish it would carry over in my absence.

Anyway, if I have had failures on the curricular frontiers, at least I have controlled and brought understanding to what might have been a volatile situation.

My students are precocious

"I wish I had a little girl guinea pig."

"Why would you like a little girl guinea pig, Tyrone?"

"Because for Granville [our little boy guinea pig]. You let him all alone here all weekend and every night. If he had a little girl guinea pig, he could play with her all day and then at night they, well, ha ha . . ."

The story of the hamsters

Our class pets, two hamsters, had grown to nine. In an effort to curb the population, I told the boys and girls that if anyone wanted one to take home, he should bring a note from mother and he could have one. The next day seven notes came back. Mary brought her note to my attention first. I was very happy because Mary was a very quiet and withdrawn little girl. In fact, she had never shown an interest to this extent in anything in the classroom before.

About some of the others I was not so happy. Nora tended to be quite careless. She would soon lose interest. Melvin's family was so poor I didn't quite know how they could be bothered with even the minimal expenses involved in keeping a hamster. Dwight's house had such a menagerie of animals in it that I couldn't understand his interest in a hamster. My fears about William's sadistic tendencies were supported by the other teachers who scoffed at William's ability to do anything but act mean. Tyrone seemed much too slow to know how to care for a hamster, and Felix was unable to keep anything safe from the destructiveness of his little brothers and sisters. The cleaning lady added to my misgivings by an emotional entreaty to give them to a pet shop where they would be cared for. But a deal is a deal, so that evening I gave the seven notebearers their hamsters.

Recently I made a point of checking with each of the hamsters' progress. Nora's had died, but from how she described her care of him, it seemed that this was not the cause of death. Her daddy was pleased with how she took care of him, too, so much so that when the hamster died he gave her a puppy, with whom she is very happy. Melvin's mother is very happy with his hamster. William has bought another hamster so he can mate them. He called to tell me that the mother destroyed the first litter, and he is trying to figure out a way to prevent this from happening the next time. Tyrone was very happy with his pet, and Felix's mother had purchased a fairly expensive cage to keep his pet safe.

But Mary? Mary took her hamster home and fed it to her pet cat!

People on welfare should not starve

The children of poverty, like their elders, constantly find contact with institutional people undermining to their self-esteem, inside and outside the classroom:

(1) Our group visited the Department of Public Welfare. Here the attitude of our guide was one of disrespect for human beings and of contempt for the poor. He made me wonder if the Department was run on the philosophy of a former classmate of mine: people on welfare should not starve but should be kept just above starvation and deprived as much as possible of self-respect as an incentive!

(2) It is common in schools, and especially in some of the core schools I saw this summer, for teachers to expect respect from the children while making it all too clear that they do not respect the kids at all.

Failure

Failure is having the art projects of the students who didn't follow directions turn out much better than the projects of those who did. Or maybe that is really the definition of success.

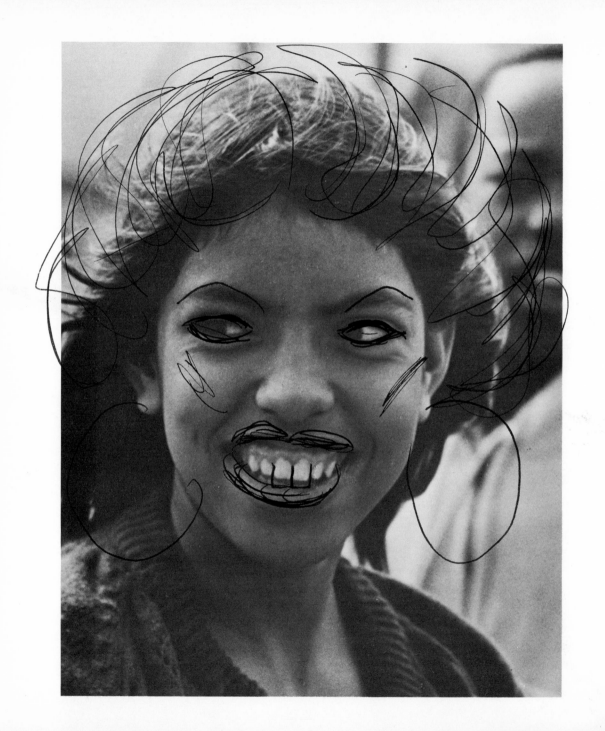

Do I understand?

The general consensus around the lunch table today was that most people on relief are lazy. They really don't care about getting a job. They prefer to live off welfare. We, as taxpayers, are suckers to support them.

One teacher referred to a case she knew. The woman receiving welfare has seven or eight children —all illegitimate. She spends most of her welfare money on liquor. She cares nothing for her children's well-being. She has publicly let it be known that she doesn't want to work—that it is easier to live off the government. Except for me, everyone at the table agreed she should be made to work and that her children should be placed in a home.

They are often very pushy

Comments from the teachers' lounge:

"Do you suppose —————— is Negro or Puerto Rican?"

"I believe she's Puerto Rican."

"That must be, she's so aggressive and demanding. There's something about that nationality. I've noticed they are often very pushy."

As the school changed, so did the faculty

A white male member of our faculty was asked what he felt were some of the current issues facing the city public schools. When he failed to mention de facto segregation, he was asked his feelings about this issue. He replied that he did not feel this was the Number One issue. He felt it had many implications but that it was only a problem in the schools that are changing (from white to black).

He taught at a school that went from zero to 75 per cent colored within a few years. The books and the building remained the same, but the "school" was not the same because the same use was not made of the facilities available. The first few years the staff remained the same, but as the "school" changed, so did the faculty. Extra activities were cut out because there was no demand for them.

The change was in the homes the children were coming from. He felt a change in the morals of the parents was the start of the problem. Whether a child goes to 13th Street School or Hill View, the home is still the most important factor. Half a child's battle is won if he has a good home. He felt it must be remembered that the home is the first educator. The school is only the second educator. His own children have no problems in school. Therefore he is satisfied. He is a strict parent.

The children in the core school where he taught fell into three groups: (1) the children coming from culturally deprived homes; (2) the "good middle"; (3) the "middle" who were increasingly influenced by the "bad half." The children in the "bad half" were able to control the classrooms because they were in the majority and could rule by fear and force. These children had no respect for themselves.

School busing: reactions in the teachers' lounge

This particular black teacher felt these children could disrupt a classroom if they were a majority. But if only a few of these problem children were placed in a room, they would have to go along with the others.

He said he felt he had found a solution to the entire problem when he was in high school. He felt that if one Negro family were placed in each block in the city, the problem would be solved.

At this point the entrance bell rang. We all thought the discussion was finally getting down to business. A white teacher in the room said she felt it took so long to get around to the point because we white teachers are shocked at first when a black teacher asks us such direct questions. The black teacher doing the questioning said she liked to discuss things out in the open. She felt anyone was free to disagree with her just as she was free to disagree with them. But she expressed doubt that her attitude was typical of the average Negro. She attended a predominantly white Catholic college and has spent most of her life with white people.

Personal thought: What is de facto segregation? I've felt it meant segregation because of neighborhood schools. One of our teachers made the statement that there is de facto segregation in anything.

I looked up "de facto" in Webster's dictionary. It is defined as: "in fact; actual (regardless of legal or moral considerations)." "Segregation" is defined as: "segregate—to set apart from others or from the main mass or group; isolate; specifically, to compel [racial groups] to live, go to school, etc., apart from each other."

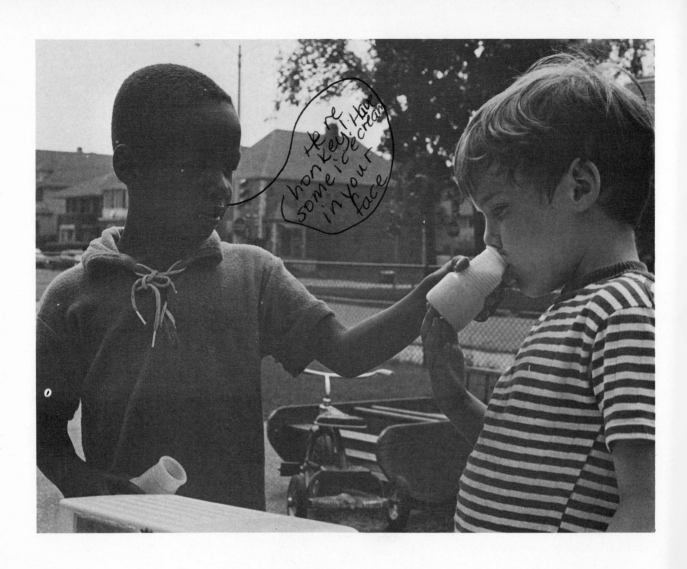

Comments of a substitute

We have a substitute teacher at our school this week who is Jewish. She commented on how conscious her eight-year-old son and his friends are of their religious backgrounds. They know if their friends are Catholic, Lutheran, Jewish, etc. Recently she overheard a conversation between her son and some of his Jewish friends. One boy asked her son if he knew another boy. When he replied "No," his friend said, "Well, you wouldn't know him anyhow because he's Lutheran."

She reflected as to how, as a child, she herself was very conscious of her Jewish background. As a child she often wondered if German children she knew felt guilty about the persecution of the Jews by Germans.

The remark prompted one of our Negro teachers to voice her views on the subject of an individual feeling guilty about the actions of other members of his race. She said while she certainly did not condone riots, neither could she feel guilty or ashamed. If she were to feel guilty and apologetic, then why shouldn't whites feel equally guilty and apologetic about the activities of the Ku Klux Klan?

I interjected that this viewpoint continued to be very revealing and thought-provoking to me. I refer to the viewpoint that just because this teacher is a Negro does not mean that she can speak or account for the actions of all Negroes. This is simple logic, but I have failed to understand it until now. Can I give the "white" viewpoint because I am Caucasian?

Make it a double scotch and go light on the questions

At a recent party a faculty wife asked this Negro teacher if she knew a particular Negro minister and Negro teacher. When she replied "No," the wife was very shocked. Just because the Negro teacher is a member of their race this woman expected her to know them. They are Negro and she is Negro—that is reason enough.

This reminded us both of a cartoon in *Ebony* magazine. It shows a Negro man at a cocktail party. He is the only Negro there, and he is surrounded by a circle of white people. The caption reads, "Let the nonwhite guest enjoy his martini before settling down to the inevitable seminar on 'the problem.' If his is a neophyte audience, make it a double scotch and go light on the questions."

"I may make whitey out of you!"
The class was relaxed from the beginning. One of the children took advantage of it and went too far. I cautioned him but he ignored me. I picked up the eraser and walked toward him. "You better be quiet. Otherwise, I may make whitey out of you," I said. Suddenly the whole class burst into laughter. Children really have a better sense of humor than some adults.

When I disagree I am silent
I mentioned to Mr. W. today that Tom and I had taken our son to Bradford Beach Saturday, Sunday, and Monday—the Fourth of July weekend. Wrinkling his nose, he—a "master" teacher with ten years of experience in an inner-city school—asked: "Hasn't that beach sort of gone to the dogs?" When I suggested he be more specific, he said, "You know, a lot of crummy people go there now."

Or answer this question:
"How come all the teachers live so far away from school?"

Time to start yoga
One of the central factors seems to be that when I'm not healthy, the class is not healthy. When I bring to school any emotional upsets, I can offer the children no stability or equanimity.

When I walk into a class feeling a little inadequate, the children sense immediately any uneasiness, restlessness.

As time passes, I come to understand the importance of maintaining a climate that is balanced, healthful, and happy. Time to start yoga.

The Teacher Corps:
an intern's first summer
A time of depression—we will fail this summer
Big Mother laying on us—suffocating us
  Mother, we been born. Let us up
  No hope till something new comes
    Biding time till the failure is completed
      and we can go on—to another failure
        —but a new one
. . . Hope, excitement at a new chance to fail
  —till the new moment of depression

A chip on her shoulder
The discussion last Tuesday evening in the teachers' lounge about the black teacher who is accused by a fellow faculty member of having "a chip on her shoulder" makes me think of some things I have observed about Jane's thinking lately. Jane and I have talked together many times about discrimination and her personal feelings. One day we happened to get around to talking about the KKK and Bogalusa, Louisiana. She told me she was born in Bogalusa and asked if I would like to know how her family had come to this city. They had been forced to leave the South because of an incident involving her younger brother. He had been beaten savagely by a drunken white man. He required plastic surgery on his face. When her mother tried to bring charges against the white man, they were told to leave town or else.
  Jane has a chip on her shoulder.

If he hollers

Can a teacher who is amused by the fact that his pupils count Negroes from the bus while on a field trip and who gives pupils a nod of approval when they gleefully tell jokes about Negroes in dialect be in fact a teacher?

He makes a game of the coat hooks

I walk down the hall to the principal's office and I hear, "Sit down!" "Get away from there." "Can't you ever behave?!" "Quiet!!" from each successive room. In the hall by each door is some child put there for punishment, but he doesn't really know why he is there, because after two minutes he's forgotten, so he makes a game of the coat hooks, or counts the buttons on his shirt. But I have never passed by without hearing shrieking soprano voices at fevered pitch of annoyance. This is teaching?

"Lady, don't you say nothin' 'bout my hair!"

I am discovering that there's a unique element in the relationship between teacher and pupil if their races are different. Yesterday I watched the English Department chairman handle a boy who was late to class because of waiting too long at the water fountain. She thought he had written "Went to the barber" as an excuse. In fact he had written "Went to the bubbler." She asked if he didn't think he could get a haircut some other time; he misunderstood, said, "Lady, don't you say nothin' 'bout my hair!" She didn't get it, replied, "Don't be insolent with me, young man." There was a heated exchange and she reminded him whom he was talking to. His reply was he didn't give a damn; of course, losing the battle, he was hauled off to the office. The student saw racial overtones that she possibly didn't, but I felt that she might have been more sensitive.

We were comfortable together

I met Anthony yesterday when I was cleaning up my car. I was busily scrubbing the upholstery when a small face peered in and said, "How's that flashlight stay up?" I showed him the small magnet that holds the flashlight to the dash, and he spent several minutes attaching the flashlight to the car's door, roof, and hood. He then read the insignia on the hood and came back to inform me that I own a Cheb-O-let. We talked about that word for a few minutes, then agreed to go read a story after finishing the car. He scrubbed my windows with the dirty sponge that had been used on the upholstery (I surreptitiously redid them later that evening), and we went for an ice cream cone. We then retired to the front stoop of his house, where, surrounded by brothers and sisters, he read a story to me. He reads well and was quite proud of himself when he learned a new word and recognized it when it reappeared. Conditions were excellent for teaching. We were comfortable together, and he was eager to demonstrate his ability to read.

A teacher of teachers

Summer school ended yesterday at 10:30. After the boys and girls had left the school building, the teacher felt obligated to give me some advice:

"Use your authority. I look at a kid who's continually misbehaved and say something to him, but at the same time I'm thinking, 'You snotty-nosed kid, listen to me. I'm an adult, and you're just a kid. What right have you to act the way you do.' "

and . . .

"The books say you shouldn't make an example of a kid before the class, but it works for me. If you call him on something he's not supposed to do and he doesn't stop, do what I do—belittle him and he'll fall in line." He then proceeded to tell me about an intern teacher he had last semester who was a virtual dictator in the classroom. With Mr. W. approving of every disciplinary tactic employed by this beginning teacher. Sitting in the back of the room, he would say something to this effect to "troublemakers":

"Who are you? Do you want special privileges? Do you want to be treated differently? Just who do you think you are? . . ." After the teacher had delivered this barrage of questions, the pupil wilted in his seat and gave the teacher no more trouble.

Mr. W. wasn't interested in or sympathetic with the inner conflicts or the lives of the children outside the classroom. Thus he treated the behavior problems encountered in a rather detached manner; the delinquent person was warned and reprimanded again and again. When I asked him how much he thought was accomplished by repeatedly reprimanding one Peter B. in our class, he pointed to a box of Kleenex with a message scrawled on it—"To Mr. W. from Peter"—and said, "No matter how rough you are on these kids throughout the year, they end up loving you at the end."

On joining the National Teacher Corps

My affluent children and their friends think that I'm a "kook," that this is a "lark." They refuse to be bothered with the other America—if I want to do this and "it makes you happy, go ahead."

I want to teach like him

We began tutoring potential failures today. I am dismayed by Mrs. Schwartz, who has seven students (class of fifteen) who are flunking. Her teaching method is: lecture, write a vague assignment on the board ("Write a theme about King Arthur's Great Idea"), and correct papers at her desk while the students supposedly do homework. I am impressed with Mr. Wilson; he's totally disorganized, and such questions as, "Where'd I leave my textbook, kids?" create brief bedlam as everyone shouts an answer, but he's careful to set the kids up for a lesson, helping them to see that their literature assignments are related to things other than an English teacher's whims. (Intro to *Caesar:* "Can you think of any countries today where a government has been overthrown? Why do people try to overthrow a government?") I want to teach like him, but I would like the order that prevails in Mrs. Schwartz's class. But, do I want an orderly classroom because it's conducive to learning—or because principals and supervisors prefer this? Mrs. Schwartz is probably regarded as the better teacher.

She is not happy where she is

The following comments were made by teachers at a bridal shower last Thursday evening. One white female teacher had quite a lot to say about her teaching experience in a core school. This is her first year of teaching. She teaches primary children, all of whom are black except for one white boy.

She is not happy teaching where she is. The children are wild and nearly impossible to teach. She spends almost all day trying to maintain some sort of order and discipline. She ends the day exhausted and defeated. She feels the children are not interested in learning. But they do like arithmetic and music and will sit still for awhile when engaged in these activities. On the other hand, they are not interested in reading. Most are still reading out of pre-primers. It is interesting to note, though, that they do not like to read from charts because charts are too "babyish" for second-graders. She has found a gimmick to teach phonics. Knowing their interest in music, she uses a drum to accompany the children while they chant sounds such as "Bah—baby—Bah—ball . . ." etc. When she does manage to establish some discipline, it is easily disrupted. The children have little self-control, and "an eye for an eye" seems the rule. For example, if Johnny cannot find his pencil he will immediately accuse his neighbor of stealing it and start beating him up. This teacher commented that she had never seen children who were so cruel to one another. They will deliberately trip anyone walking down the aisle.

The only means of maintaining discipline that she feels works is physical punishment. This view is shared by her principal and fellow teachers. She said she was shocked at first to see teachers carrying wooden paddles, but after only a few months she feels she could use one. She has been told not to be afraid to use a paddle but to be careful not to break the skin. Otherwise it's just the child's word against the teacher's that he has been hit by a paddle. This use of physical force is justified because "this is the only thing these kind of children understand." One of the other teachers interrupted and asked how the children were supposed to learn anything else if force was always used in school. The core teacher replied again that this was the way things were done

in the home and the school can't change the home. At this point the conversation switched to another topic.

My reactions and thoughts: Throughout the entire conversation I had the feeling I was hearing things I had heard before: "Negro children do not want to learn." "Physical force is the only thing these kind of children understand." "The trouble is in the home." "The school can't change the home."

I do not deny that this teacher is having a difficult time. Any teacher's first year is difficult, and certainly problems are increased in a core school. Nor do I deny that this teacher is trying to do a good job. In fact, I feel she is a creative teacher and is really trying to do her best. The sad thing is that she is not really prepared to teach inner-city children, and she is not receiving any constructive advice on how to teach them. She herself admitted that her college courses did not prepare her for anything like this. She is shocked and at the same time amused by the coarse language the children use.

Even more unfortunate is the change that is taking place in her own mind. I feel sure she came to this job with a much more open mind than she will have when she gets her transfer. Instead of becoming less prejudiced, she is becoming more and more convinced of prejudices which she may have held or heard. By not being properly prepared and advised, she is becoming more convinced that Negro children do not want to learn—that Negroes are vulgar, coarse, etc. She fails to understand that these children have not learned how to learn; that the school can be a social force in the community, and that wooden paddles will not teach self-discipline.

Yes, I know I must sound like I know it all. Well, I don't, and very often I feel like I am standing on the outside throwing stones. This is why I am considering asking for a transfer to a core school. But I have had some experience teaching in Head Start, and I cannot help but feel that using wooden paddles is no way to handle children. This teacher admitted that her physical punishment is not working. She explained how she can take the hands of the worst boy in the room and press them together as hard as she can and he will only laugh. When she stops, he will smile and say, "Hi-ya, teacher."

A teacher's poem

The B's and V's
Don't come out right
You turn your back
Punch! There's a fight.

Ask questions? Not a
Word they'll say,
Bid "Quiet" and
They'll gab all day.

But just before
You drain the cup
A puckish one
Can break you up.

"I dig you, teacher,"
So offhand,
One-to-one,
We understand.

Donald

When Donald arrived, a transfer from Neal Street School, Mrs. S. said, "I told you that we would get problem children because we do not have a full quota of children." I looked at Donald; he seemed to confirm a prediction of trouble. He had a shifty look; he was rather badly dressed and not too clean; about him was an aura of hopelessness, combined with a feeling that while he might not get anywhere, he was going to make plenty of trouble on his way to drowning in anonymity.

Now it is some weeks later. Donald is one of the most cooperative children in the room. His whole appearance has changed. He is quiet and seems to have acquired self-esteem. When I ask him to do something he will do it willingly and completely, no matter how long or how hard it may seem. His concentration on any work task (such as an art project) is complete, and he does not stop until he has really finished.

I was told that he has poor hearing. Yet I never have to repeat anything to him.

He stands straight and tall. He smiles. He is happy. How did it happen? Affection, trust, and approval.

Since the teacher refused to treat him as a potential delinquent, but instead as a potential success, he is living up to expectations, and beyond.

He knows his teacher cares; he knows he can depend on someone; so he gives back the same.

School boycott

White Male Teacher: Senseless—does nothing for the child—does not improve the Negro image—a school boycott is defiance of the law—we have courts of law in which they can voice their demands.

Negro Mother and Teacher: I do not agree with the boycott. My husband and I plan to take our children to school in the morning—take them home for lunch—take them back and pick them up after school.

School Secretary: It is terrible. What is it doing for the child? How can we teach them to respect the law by disobeying it? What do we have laws for if we are going to break them? What are these children going to learn? It is harmful to the children. There must be some other way to handle the problem. Part of it is their fault and then, too, part of it is our fault.

Minister: I am against the boycott because it teaches disrespect for the law. These problems of de facto segregation should be solved in our courts.

Female Negro Teacher: I thought I knew what de facto segregation was. Now I'm not sure. Doesn't it mean segregation because of housing patterns? Integrating bused-in classes would be difficult administratively. Busing merely to integrate a school is not a good thing. I'm against it.

White Teacher: I always was against integrating bused-in classes because we never did it at our school. I always thought it would be difficult to keep records. But now after really thinking about it, I don't think it would be a problem.

Another White Teacher: If I moved to a nice neighborhood and was told my daughter would have to attend school in the core, I wouldn't do it! Every parent buys a home in a particular area because he wants his children to attend the school in that area. Wouldn't you be compounding these children's personal defects by putting them into a class with good ones?

White Male Teacher: If people such as civil rights groups want to present their case, let them put it in the form of a referendum. Let the voters decide. Let them get together with the school board and other civic leaders and discuss rather than argue. There seems to be a lack of communication. A survey of teachers' opinions would be a good thing. No one has asked the teachers. Groups such as civil rights groups do not represent the Negro people. Negroes who did not go along with the last boycott were intimidated by those in favor of it. This is part of their basic problem—they don't even respect each other.

School Engineer: Have you heard the papers are changing the word "Negro" to "Negroid?" You know why? Because Negroid rhymes with hemorrhoid and they're both a pain in the ass.

Was he white?

After several complaining remarks about my supervisor (who is really very kind but often receives the short end of my patience), Gladys asked me, "Is he colored?" How often that question arises! Did you ever take inventory of the kind of remark that will occasion that question? And then, note too that it is phrased, "Is he colored?" With the expectancy "Yes," not "what race or nationality is he?" which allows a variety of answers. His question brought to mind a little joke I had with a few of my younger friends in the office. They'd come in and tell me about a purse snatching or some such. With a shifty glance and a rasping voice, I'd whisper, "Was he white?" And they'd howl with laughter. The black kids seem to appreciate it more, for apparently they too have been victims of the question and enjoy hearing it turned around for a change.

Teacher's house

"Teacher, is it true you live in an apartment?'

"Yes. What did you think?"

"I thought you lived in a house."

"What kind of a house?"

"Oh, I don't know. A nice house."

"Was it a wooden house or a brick house?"

"A brick house, a big brick house with a yard bigger than this room."

"Was it a two-family brick house?"

"No, it was a big brick house and you lived there all alone."

"What was it like inside, Tony?"

"Oh, I never got inside. I just thought about the outside."

Do I believe what I say?

Yesterday our principal's wife brought the junior choir she directs to our school to sing Christmas carols. They are all Negroes.

Last year the sixth grades wanted to have them stay after their singing for milk and cookies. Our principal said no, because he wanted to get them out before they could cause any trouble. Jane asked me at lunch last week if I would ask the principal if the teachers could at least extend the invitation to the choir to stay for refreshments. She felt this would be a good way to foster good relations between our white children and these colored children. She did not want to ask because she is a Negro and knows how our principal feels. She was unaware of the remark made by our principal last year. Putting my foot in my big mouth, I told her what he had said. The expression on her face made me wish I had not told her. I said I would ask him, but I did not think they would have enough time to stay. I did feel we should extend the invitation, however.

They were here yesterday and no invitation was made. Sure, I can rationalize my reasons for doing nothing. In fact, I can even list them:

(1) His wife would have said no anyway.

(2) He would have said no immediately.

(3) I forgot because I was so busy with testing, writing a paper, and with Christmas.

(4) I voiced a contrary opinion to my principal a few weeks ago and met stony, firm resistance. After all, I want to stay on the good side of him.

(5) My husband does not share my views about the Negro. If I had asked and gotten myself into trouble, I would have had to face the music at home.

On the surface the above sound like good reasons —but looking deeper they seem quite superficial. They are loaded with "ifs." It boils down that I just did not have enough guts! In the future, will I do the same or will I be able to put into action what I say in words?

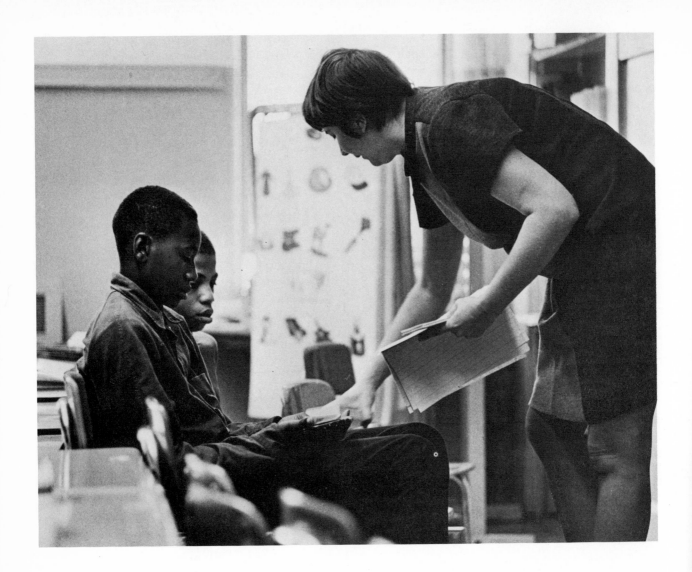

J.D.'s problem

What are we going to do with J.D.? J.D.'s Daddy comes home from work at 10:30 p.m., after J.D. has gone to bed. He gets up again some time after J.D. leaves for school. He cares for J.D., calls home at 6:00 p.m. to see that J.D. is eating the supper he has prepared for him and again at 9:00 p.m. to see that J.D. has returned home from play. J.D. sees Daddy a few hours on Saturday when they clean the house together and on Sunday when they play checkers or go bike riding or watch television. J.D. is forever speaking of Daddy. His spelling sentences sing Daddy's praises. In J.D.'s comparisons of Daddy to his teacher, teacher runs a poor second. J.D.'s mother? Down south. J.D. used to dream of killing her but now speaks of her indifferently. J.D. will not get married ever. Why not? Because if you get married, your wife will run around with other men and cause trouble. Do all wives run around with other men or do just some of them? Most of them do!

A sundae for Jimmy

Jimmy had come over for supper with us that evening. Midway during the meal, I apologized to him that we would not have dessert but added that we could stop for a sundae when we drove him home.

"Sunday? What's a sunday?"

"You know, Jimmy, ice cream with chocolate syrup, whipped cream, nuts, and things on top."

"Ohhh—I don't think I'd like that!"

I wonder

I drove Miss P. home. She told me of an FBI man in her apartment building, who told her that Martin Luther King was a known Communist (this was three hours before he was assassinated). When I protested that it was ridiculous, that he was a man of the cloth and interested in peace and right, she vehemently insisted that his whole history was known, and he really was a Communist (I capitalize it because that's the kind she intimated he was). When I said, "No FBI man would reveal any information," she replied, "These are things that are known." And we went on to talk of draperies, which really interested her because she is decorating a new apartment.

I gave her credit for being broader minded than she is. She's a good teacher—and that's all she has to be in our school. But how much do the closed, narrow opinions of a teacher affect the class? Do they antagonize? After all, subject matter is not the end—she teaches subject matter very well and is fair and insists on what is moral and ethical . . .

What smooch means

"Oh, teacher, that word 'smooch' is a bad word."

"I thought it just meant kiss."

"Oh, no. It's bad."

"Well, would you say it in front of your mother?"

"Nooo, teacher. I'll tell you what it means. You know those hamsters you have?"

"Yes."

"You know that one's a mama and the other's a papa?"

"Yes."

"Remember the mama had seven babies?"

"Yes."

"Well, you know what started those babies, don't you, teacher?"

"Yes."

"Well, that's smooch!"

Smooch to Tony

"I like girls. I like to smooch with them."

"Isn't 'smooch' a bad word, Tony?"

"No, that ain't a bad word. All it means is kiss."

Dust

"Carol, do you have a nickel?"

"Nickel?"

"Yes, nickel! Did you bring your nickel?"

"Nickel? You mean what you spend?"

"Yes. Nickel. Money. Dust!"

"Oh! Yes! Why didn't you say so?"

George Washington Jones, Grover Cleveland, Timothy McCarthy, and Charles Dickens Powell

At lunch today I was speaking to several friends about one of my students, whose name is Elizabeth Taylor Carson. "Oh, she *must* be colored," they chorused happily. She is, but oh how I would have loved to have told them she wasn't. Oh to have seen their smugness wither into that mild shame that hits a face that is caught in a small mistake. Instead I told them of four friends of mine, George Washington Jones, Grover Cleveland, Timothy McCarthy, and Charles Dickens Powell, and asked them to identify their races.

A trick—and they fell, hook, line, and sinker. Timothy is black, the other three are white, and only one of them from the South, so there! And besides, I think Elizabeth Taylor is a beautiful name. Frequently when speaking of Grover Cleveland in the past, I had been asked if he were colored. Sometimes when mentioning his name I could see the question forming on my one-man audience's face and would say, "No, he's not colored!," which was an insultingly pleasant way of correcting a misconception.

I hate you

> You can make me do things
> I don't want to do;
> I hate to do things;
> I hate you.

One of the teachers I know made up this poem to express the feelings of one of the boys in her class. The little boy wanted the teacher to read the poem over and over again; and when he had heard it enough he gave her a hug and jumped off her lap chanting the poem.

The only way to teach

Parents, especially those who have limited education, are only aware of a child's learnings through (1) lots of homework, (2) rigid "seatwork," preferably printed sheets, (3) "good" or "bad" marks on assignments, (4) "hard" arithmetic (borrowing, carrying, large numbers, etc.). They see no value in the child's learning to think, generalize, or conceptualize through his lessons . . . In other words, they value the rigid teachers, following patterns that were prevalent long ago.

Some teachers, certainly those who use such methods, believe that this is the only way to teach. These teachers are looked on as model teachers. They get the best students. Practice teachers are always placed with them.

Administrators respect them more, at least principals do. They seem to follow all rules exactly, promptly. They never digress or dissent. They follow a cut and dried, very efficient pattern.

Black justice

Several months ago a playful fight was taking place between four Negro children. One shouted gleefully, "Let's give him [one of the boys] Black Justice." The three proceeded to pounce on the fourth boy. They all walked away pals.

Dr. King

Dr. Martin Luther King got shot in Memphis.
He is in the hospital.
He got shot in the neck by a bullet.
We going to marching.

(*Third Grade*)

April 5, 1968

Dear Mrs. King,
    I am very sorry that had to happen.
I hope they catch the man who shot your husbean.
I thing that he is the greatest man on earth.
May god for give the killer.
I am truly sorry.
        Sincerely, Valeava Allen
        Age 8

Teacher's joke

"Did you hear they caught King's killer?"

"Yeah."

"They fined him $20 for shootin' 'coon out of season."

A summer tan

Alfred stopped by this afternoon. We walked over to the art center. On the way I happened to mention how much sun I had been getting and that my arms were really tan. Alfred replied that a tan was something he sure didn't need. Jokingly I added that he had the same summer status color, to which he replied, "Boy, it sure don't do no good in the wintertime."

Skin

The phenomenon of skin is continuing to provide delight. The children enjoy pressing my skin which turns white and then back to the tan shade.

They watch and remark daily as the sun "sinks in" to my skin.

And the greatest fascination and horror has been my peeling. I didn't realize how foreign this was to the children, for when they saw me peel they wanted to rush me to the hospital—"Where does the skin go?" "Are you a snake?" "Can we live without skin?"

Not only did I have a nice vacation, but it was a wonderful learning experience for all concerned.

Elvin's problem

"Teacher, can a man train his dog to bite just certain people or to bite just one man?"

"What do you mean, Elvin?"

"Well, could a man train his dog to bite just a black man? You see, there was a story in the paper about this man and he had this dog and he trained this dog to bite and chase all black people."

"Oh, I see. Well, I think what this fellow did was to train the dog to bite anyone that the man would sic the dog after. And when he had the dog trained, he would sic him after black people. But the dog didn't choose. Dogs can't tell black people from white people as far as I know."

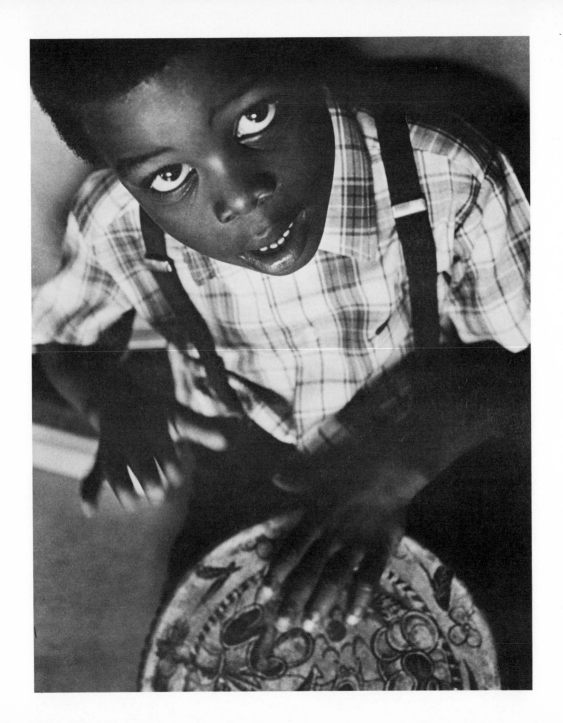

Beethoven

"Our lesson today, boys and girls, is about a man with a long name, Ludwig von Beethoven. Has anyone ever heard or seen this name or know anything about Beethoven?"

"Oh, just another famous Negro!"

Dialect

"Our teacher she always say pick up the floor now, but she really mean sweep it."

Image

"I remember once this white kid at our school . . ."

"There were never any white kids at our school!" A rude interruption.

"Yes, there was!"

"No, there weren't, were there, teacher? Were there any white kids around here?"

"Well, some years ago there were lots of white kids in our school . . ."

"But they all moved out, didn't they?" The first voice again.

"Yes! I wonder why they moved away . . ."

"Why because we moved here," came the first speaker again. "They didn't want to live with us messy niggers."

Tolerance

"Oh, I don't mind white kids. They smell funny though!"

Overheard in the corridor

". . . and then we got where there was no more colored people, just me, and I was scared."

June

June, a student I'm tutoring, told me today why she never speaks up in class (the reason for the referral for tutoring). She is deaf in one ear—can hardly hear the teacher. I wonder how many like June are never discovered. The condition could have been corrected when she was a little girl in Georgia, but her mother couldn't afford the treatment. She's been shipped out to a cousin; twelve brothers and sisters remain in Atlanta. A recent composition tells much about June: "You can't depend on no one," she writes.

Florice and Andy

Today Florice became ill while in school, and I sent her up to the nurse. The nurse asked her if mother was home. She said, "Yes, but Mama doesn't feel good." When asked what was wrong, she replied, "Oh, she went out last night and got a little bitty drunk." Florice is five years old and already knows that her mother suffers when she goes out and gets drunk. Florice was ill when she came to school in the morning. She should have stayed home, but her mother probably felt too bad herself to worry about her.

I'm sure that administrators and teachers in suburbia have the same problem to handle. Perhaps the "illness" is more easily concealed. When I practice-taught at a suburban nursery school, several children were emotionally disturbed and handicapped by this same problem—parental neglect. I particularly remember one little boy, Andy, who was extremely disturbed. He had three teen-age brothers and a mother and father who were far too busy with business and social affairs to bother with him. But he did have a colored Nanny who was both mother and father to him. He was well fed and clothed. Both he and his parents were under psychiatric care. All this, of course, costs money, and this was one thing his parents had lots of and were willing to give.

Deviant behavior by children such as Florice more often is labeled as "naughty, troublesome, bad, what-is-to-be-expected-of-people-like-them"—while the "Andys" of the upper and middle classes are not naughty but emotionally disturbed.

Who is more neglected? Who will make the better adjustment—Florice or Andy?

Two hundred kids gathered outside the school

A considerable number of students were absent today because of yesterday's events. By 12:00 most of the white kids (who made the mistake of coming in the morning) had checked out. There were no white kids in my afternoon classes. All day long white kids and teachers were getting eggs shot at them by a small number of troublemakers. I was lucky and didn't have this problem. Many of the teachers drove home the few white kids who stayed for the day's length, so that they wouldn't have to walk through the neighborhood.

Immediately after school about two hundred kids gathered outside the school, milled around, and then moved to a city playground only a half-block away. (We watched from the school windows.) . . . Suddenly, rocks and bottles at passing cars. In a minute or so the kids surged into the street and trapped a car. Then an interesting thing happened. The whole mob suddenly appeared confused. They had a white man trapped in his stopped car but couldn't figure out what to do next. At this time several of us men teachers (most of them Negro) were approaching the kids to see if we could help quiet down the situation. The trapped car had begun to inch forward, and the kids began to yell and pound on the windows. Two of them ripped off one part of the chrome tail-fin. Upon hearing this the driver panicked and shot forward. Miraculously he missed everyone, although several kids flew to the pavement to avoid him. In a few seconds the mob realized that "Whitey had escaped with everything and was probably laughing." More rocks into the street. I'm standing about forty feet from the group. I see an egg splatter on the curb near me . . . I now realize that perhaps the few white teachers are about to become targets of their wrath. Henry Heller—my team leader (a Negro)—comes up to me and says that unless I can turn black in about ten seconds, I better fade away. At that moment there is a smash, then another smash—a four-car accident at the intersection. Two cars, both trying to avoid the kids and rocks, sideswipe each other. A third car bounces up the curb and into the school fence. A fourth vehicle—a truck—hits the curb so hard that his tire blows out. All the kids are now screaming and scurrying about. The drivers of the cars climb out. All of them are black. For a moment the noise subsides. One of the drivers is the wife of a Negro teacher who has been out here all the while. Now a squad car arrives along with a motorcycle officer. The whole situation is bewildering. Who's to blame? No one knows! Suddenly all the kids take off. Just like a vast herd they bolt down 20th Street toward Main.

It grows quiet. Why did the kids leave? One of the teachers who was watching from his third-floor window now comes out and says that he could see about ten or fifteen white kids at the end of the block. That's who the mob began to chase. I decide to leave. I open the car door. My briefcase bounces on the back seat. I turn the ignition key and my motor coughs to life . . .

As I drive home I remember a statement of Ausubel. At home I look it up. "Increased physical contact per se between white and Negro children does little to reduce prejudice, but more intimate personal interaction under favorable circumstances significantly reduces social distance between the two groups."

Two occasions of hard reality

I played my guitar for a Head Start class this morning, and they stared at me as if they all played the guitar or as if I were strumming their mothers. It was like a reaction I got at a party once at 2 a.m. after everyone had gotten stoned. Maybe class stimulation means sobering up the group. This means figuring out the normal state of a five-year-old child at a particular time and place. There was a temptation merely to shout.

I went on a field trip last week with a class and walked home in a huddle of four or five girls. They were polite in talking in turn, but now (and even right after the trip) I can't remember anything any of them said.

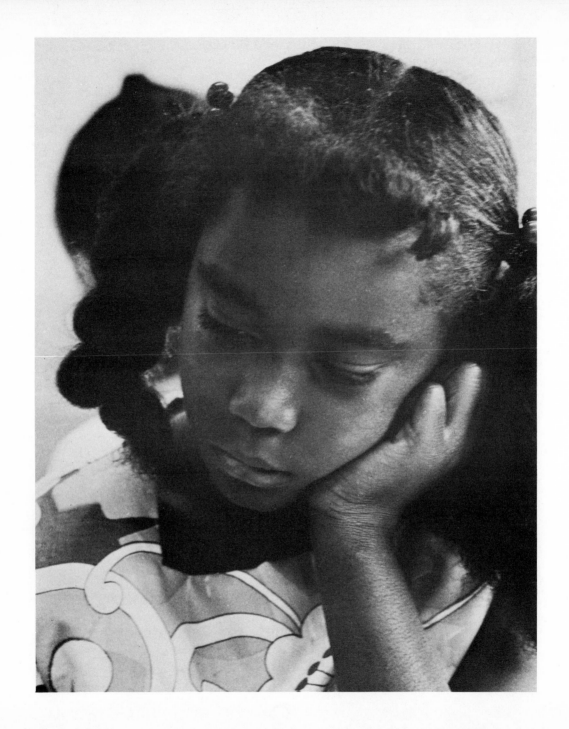

Elsie

One little girl, Elsie, became a little tired early this morning and was obviously unhappy. Miss O. discovered that the family had a party the night before. Mr. W. discovered that there were thirteen children at home. As the morning progressed, Elsie became increasingly unhappy.

Each of us read a great deal into Elsie's behavior, until about noon a tooth fell from her mouth.

Dream

Scene: The main office of an inner-city school.

Sequence of events: In the last hour the students have taken over the school.

Interesting sidelight: The principal is on his knees holding a tablet of paper in one hand while with the other he writes: "The schools therefore should aim at controlling or disciplining student by *rewards* rather than by punishments."

The student leader who has taken his place has told the dethroned principal that he must write that Patricia Sexton quote two hundred times and then submit to five paddle swats . . .

In the bakery shop

Today I entered the bakery just in time to hear an older man expound on what he would do if ever any of those "black bastards" tried anything on him. What really angered me was the way he looked at me, so confident of my moral support of his feelings. In a sense it was quite a pathetic scene. The voice began losing its firmness and self-confidence as I continued to glare at him, and he discovered he was talking to someone who had no sympathy or feeling for his cause. One gets so sick and tired of trying to reason with people who defend their stands by emotions that I had simply resorted to a glare. Perhaps it was more effective than discourse, for a glare is an emotional thing, a meeting on the same level.

Newspapers take a great delight in this sort of thing . . .

Did you ever notice the need a speaker has to tell his audience when a character in his narrative is black? Miss P. did it tonight when she told us about the impoverished home she visited with all the little Negro children on the floor. She said nothing about them, their age, size, type of clothing, nothing except that they were colored. Yet this fact had absolutely no bearing on her story. It would have been exactly the same story had the family been white.

Newspapers take great delight in this sort of thing: The assailant, John Smith, a Negro. The picture makes that obvious. Wouldn't it look funny to see: The assailant, John Jones, a white man?

A glimmer of hope

"Ruby told me you wanted to see me, Jim." "Yes, I wanted to ask you about your year in Mississippi." "It was rough." I hoped by vague remarks like this to avoid a painful subject. He wouldn't be satisfied with vagueness. His questions became more and more specific and so too my answers, always with an attempt to make them as painless as possible, as truthful as possible. This is difficult! Jim is fifteen, but do people stop feeling pain at fifteen? If my psychology courses stand me well, it would seem logical that capacity for pain increases as one grows in knowledge and wisdom and age. I told him many Southerners hated Yankees and Catholics and Jews, too, but I didn't tell him the hatred for these groups was much less intense. I didn't tell him our black janitor was known to my classmates as "black son of a bitch," and that as a Yankee I was given a special reminder of this because they figured that in my Yankee stupidity I might call him by his Christian name. Christian name—how that phrase sticks to my pen when I recall this incident—how unlike the teachings of this Christ, a member himself of a minority group and despised in almost all its history. And now I think of Eustace (black son of a bitch) pulling light bulbs and paper cups and other refuse out of those commodes back in Jackson. Has the Emancipation Proclamation, Fourteenth Amendment, Reconstruction, World War II, Supreme Court decision, civil rights legislation affected your life at all, Eustace? Have you heard of them at all? No, but he has heard that those Northern Negroes are sure getting the Southern niggers in a mess of trouble. A glimmer of hope!

Do something useful with your life

Mom and Dad were down for a visit. "You need a haircut, a new pair of pants, and I hope you're steering clear of those civil rights agitators! Do something useful with your life. Get into something with a steady income. The NAACP won't support you." Silence . . .

Jenice: she wasn't wild and didn't snap her fingers . . .

I first met Jenice in June 1962, between my junior and senior years at a University of Wisconsin office where we both had jobs for three months. She was hired without an interview beforehand, because the girl whose place she was taking had recommended her very highly. We were all quite surprised to learn that Jenice was a Negro, for the other girl hadn't mentioned this fact to anyone, although none of the other employees were Negro. My own surprise was not a result of the fact that she was the only Negro in the office; I was surprised that Betty, the girl who had left her job—a girl I considered prim, rather unimaginative, and concerned with herself— accepted Jenice and hadn't thought it was necessary to alert anyone to the fact that Jenice was a Negro. In other words, I considered Betty to be a person with an unyielding, narrow-minded set of values and therefore probably thought of all nonprejudiced persons as enlightened, aggressive people.

I think knowing Jenice rid me of many of my preconceived opinions about *all Negroes*. She wasn't "wild" and didn't snap her fingers to records and didn't wear gaudy clothes; she was domestically inclined—as I never could be or will be, I'm afraid. She cooked elegant dishes for friends and roommates every night—not just fried chicken, but recipes from magazines and newspapers. In short, she was charming and sensitive, and after knowing her I no longer think in terms of *all Negroes* possessing or not possessing certain traits or goals. She is also the first Negro I knew well enough to become interested in for herself—not because she was black or not black.

Kenneth, brother of Curtis

We have taken into the classroom Kenneth, brother of the notorious, ubiquitous Curtis, who is the subject of so much conversation in the teachers' lunchroom.

Kenneth has a visual problem—in fact, I suspect he is so nearsighted that he is almost blind (this is with thick glasses). It has given him a chip on his shoulder—he's sure at first that he hasn't seen something. He must have been badly indulged at home because of this disability, and his world seems to consist only of him and his whims.

He was sent to us by a teacher who cannot handle him and has already branded him as delinquent and impossible. (She told us that another child in the room is a kleptomaniac, and she had to search him everyday. We have had not one indication of such behavior—he participates and shares, and takes absolutely nothing.) Having been branded by his brother's behavior, and his own, Kenneth is being watched carefully. All I found was a child whose world is a foggy one—his outlines are very dim, and he was hungering for direction. When I made the rules plain to him, in a firm manner, he accepted them readily.

A note from home

Dear. Teacher.

how yov. i am Charles mother i had a call yestrsday
come in and talk with yov   i been sick with my back
for some time but today i fell a little Better. And
look. tomorrow when yov all come off Trip i will be
standing there waiting to talk with yov. i could not
make to day because i have goo and get my eyes test

Thank Yov

Mrs. Green

You'll have to get a darker tan

"In order to live on that side of town, you'll have to
get a darker tan," said a neighbor relaxing
comfortably. "You going to live with the coloreds!"
exclaimed a young boy with an inquisitive,
disbelieving stare. "Be sure to take a lot of bug
killer," was another comment. "Don't park your car
on the street; it won't survive the night," was
another.

"You is prejudiced"

I guess I expected the phone call, for I was upset about the slipshod way I had handled the problem over the winter slacks and the fifth-grade girls who claimed them.

The white girl brought a note from her mother reinforcing her claim, while the Negro girl could identify the apparel to the hemstitching. I wrote both mothers a second time, asking the white mother to bring the slacks to school. She did not.

My wife washed the supper dishes as I listened to the measured tones on the phone. "Those are my Rose's slacks, Mr. Glaris. You is prejudiced. The other mothers say so too." The back of my neck warmed, and my frustrations concerning the incident crystallized into bristling hostility. I fussed righteously at her for a moment, and hung up, cracking down the receiver.

"If that's the same woman, hang up on her!" I shouted to my wife as she moved to answer the persistent rings. She listened a moment to high-pitched words I could hear across the room, then slowly hung up.

Fuming, coat unbuttoned, I left my wife standing anxiously in the kitchen and stalked to the car. I parked on Mead Street where several children I knew from school were playing in the street, and they led me with sober curiosity to the correct address.

She was not surprised to see me. She gasped for breath as she described the slacks, the devious strategies of the white girl's mother, and my overt and blatant hate for Negroes. Her heart was bad, she said, and she shouldn't be upset. For an hour I listened to the injustices I had wrought.

I tried again to get the slacks. They were never brought to school.

Playground incident

An incident that happened to me in school still rings in my ears and is etched in my memory. I was on duty in the girls' yard. Suddenly I heard a piercing scream from hundreds of girls' voices. I went over: in the center of a huge circle of screaming girls there lay what looked like a plucked chicken. I went over, picked it up by its legs (it was a wild game bird, pheasant or quail, that someone had shot out of season), and carried it to the custodian, followed by the stream of screaming girls. It was like an incident out of a nightmare, or an existential novel, and I can never forget it.

The thirteen ghosts

I asked the class if they'd like to put on a television show. They were immediately interested, and a play evolved—they chose *The 13 Ghosts,* made up the lines and situations, and presented it beautifully at Open House.

Two Announcers: "This is station WIZ, Room 28, presenting *The 13 Ghosts.* First scene is the Smiths's house. They are having a birthday party."

Mr. Smith, Richard, and Mary, sitting on the floor in a bare house. Mrs. Smith brings in a birthday cake. Richard blows out the candles. Everyone in the class joins them in singing "Happy Birthday." Richard: "I wish we had a better house, with nice furniture, and lots of money."

Then comes a knock on the door. Mr. Smith opens it, and there is a man who introduces himself as the lawyer, Mr. Carter. Mr. Smith ushers him in and introduces him to the family. Mr. Carter is given a chair, and he informs the family that "Uncle Ebenezer has left you his house and everything in it and all his money."

Announcers: "This is scene two. The Smiths are going to their new house."

The Smiths knock on the door, which is opened by the maid, who was dusting. Mr. Smith: "We have come to live here. Uncle Ebenezer left us this house and everything in it and all his money."

Maid: "Come in, but you'll be sorry—this house is haunted."

Mr. Smith: "I don't believe in ghosts. We will stay here."

They come in and are seated by the maid, Elaine, around a table.

Maid: "We have a ouija board here, and you can prove by it that there are ghosts here."

She puts the ouija board on the table and they ask the first question, "Are there any ghosts here?" Y-E-S they spell out. "How many?" 1-3-13! "Will they hurt us?" Y-E-S.

Mr. Smith: "We're not afraid."

Maid: "You'll see for yourself when you go to sleep."

Announcers: "This is scene three. The Smiths are asleep in their new home."

The Smiths are shown asleep. (Two chairs put together for each bed—and the mother and daughter sleep next to each other—these are eleven-year-olds. The son and father each have their own bed.)

The ghosts come in, singing a song: "We are ghosts—woo—oo—oo—oo—We have come to get you. Woo—oo—oo—We have come to kill you!"

Mr. Smith, jumping up: "We're not afraid of you! Get out of here!"

Maid (who is really a witch): "If you're not afraid of us, we will leave. But first, we will do a dance for you."

And everyone joins in doing the Hokey Pokey.

Nothing else to do

Dan Johnson told me this morning that he was back on probation. He had been off probation for three days. He had gotten in with his old crowd and had broken into another house. It seems that he couldn't find anything else to do. In class Dan has improved so much in the last few weeks that I thought for sure he would keep out of trouble for some time, but he got mixed up with his old crowd again.

I know how the teacher feels

I observed a seventh-hour class of another teacher—
a two-year veteran. He had little control. It was a
bad class. One boy was frequently out of his seat
and twisting the arm of a girl across the room. Every
few moments the teacher would charge a few feet
and the boy would run back to his seat and smirk. It
was awful to see. My sympathy is with the teacher
. . . even though the kids are also victims. I know
how the teacher feels. He probably goes home at
night and tries to forget, but I wonder if he always
can. I can't. . . .

No one is teaching them anything

They did it again. The heroic little freedom fighters
. . . tore up the school. They turned over tables in
the cafeteria and broke windows on the inside of the
building. They paraded around singing "We Shall
Overcome." No one even knows exactly why they
did it this time. From my afternoon classes I learned
that the ultimate goal of a few warriors is to burn
down the school. Their rationale is that if they burn
the old structure to the pavement, the city will have
to build a new one. The kids say that no one is
teaching them anything. I didn't argue with them. In
my heart I realize they have a valid point. I myself
am convinced that educationally this junior high has
become very feeble.

Saturday

Today it is Saturday. I stayed in bed until 9:00, then I got up, washed, shaved, and made myself breakfast—scrambled eggs, sweet rolls, and bacon. Later on I will type out two or three poems and send them out—rejection slip candidates . . . Today it is Saturday . . . Tonight my wife and I will go out with another couple, probably to a movie—one with Sidney Poitier. Today and tomorrow I will recover and prepare for next week—a tournament.

Today it is Saturday, Saturday, Saturday.
I wish that Saturday
lasted for 168 hours.

Neanderthal men?

I heard that a homeroom teacher (a very attractive and vital Negro woman) whaled the hell out of about seven of the kids with her wooden pointer because of all the trouble they have been giving the teachers. They were very subdued through most of my class today . . .

Where did it all begin? Who first used physical force in an educational situation? Neanderthal men? Peking men?

They sure screwed up education. It makes it so much harder for teachers who are not oriented to physical punishment. I know that it solves nothing—physical punishment in a classroom. It merely delays explosions and disruptions. It never dissolves them or works to heal the causes of these problems.

Soul?

"Boys and girls, what does it mean to be a Soul Brother?"

"That means you're black, teacher."

"Well, what does it mean if someone says that someone has a lot of soul?"

"That means he's real black!"

What they get instead

Mrs. P. had a "superior" attitude about herself. Her life had consisted of the "right crowd," country club, correct home location, fashionable clothes and jewelry and hairdo. She was given the job to teach Negro youngsters in the core area. What cruelty! How she inflicted her hate on them, on the poor kids! She drove them further within themselves.

But really, she didn't know what harm she had caused. Not having any sensitivity or feeling for them (or perhaps, anyone), she "baby-sat" each day.

They have always said that the worst teachers are in the core schools. I never could buy that—but the longer I am here, the more I understand what is meant. Not all bad teaching, but such women! These poor kids need patient, quiet but firm teachers, and a structured, happy day. What they get instead are shrieking neurotics who put more fear into them and obstruct any learning. I'm sure I would turn off these nags myself if I were in their classrooms (in fact, I do now, in the teachers' lunchroom).

Immediate gratification

I believe it is FEAR that hinders the learning of these children. Fear of the teacher; fear of the white man; fear of their own feelings; fear of their home situations; fear that they are already failures; fear of punishment; fear of their peers; fear of the strange (dogs, large animals, rats, and a great multitude of unknowns such as ghosts, superman characters, and others that I cannot even imagine); they are obsessed by fear. Their only outlet is what is called immediate gratification—candy, punching someone, getting ahead in line, getting the biggest piece, being first, me, me, me!

Their accusations are often discourteous

I am very impressed with the quality of articulation demonstrated by both the parent and student leaders. I have no doubt that the real catalysts of change are not the teachers and administrators but the students themselves. Perhaps this is really as it should be. The whole current of history seems to show that change only occurs when the victims of injustice revolt. The kids and the parents of Jefferson School are victims . . . and they are revolting . . . their accusations are often discourteous, perhaps even unjust, but they are beginning to stimulate more new thinking at Jefferson this year than has probably been done in the last ten years.

Educational leadership

Time to prepare for Monday . . . A few minutes ago I had a thought and so I went to Bruner's *Process of Education*. On pages 18 and 19 he advises that the curriculum must be thought out and planned by the *experts* in the field. This is contradictory to what is happening in the schools. The experts have been backed into a narrow corner and have (I think through their own apathy or inexpertise) allowed the parents and kids to begin dictating the changes that they themselves should have more forcefully supported.

"You better not go there"

"Teacher, you need a haircut." (After only six weeks!)

"Yes, I know."

"Why don't you go across the street to Jenkins and get it cut?" This from Ronald.

From Tony, "He's a white man."

"That's right! You better not go there."

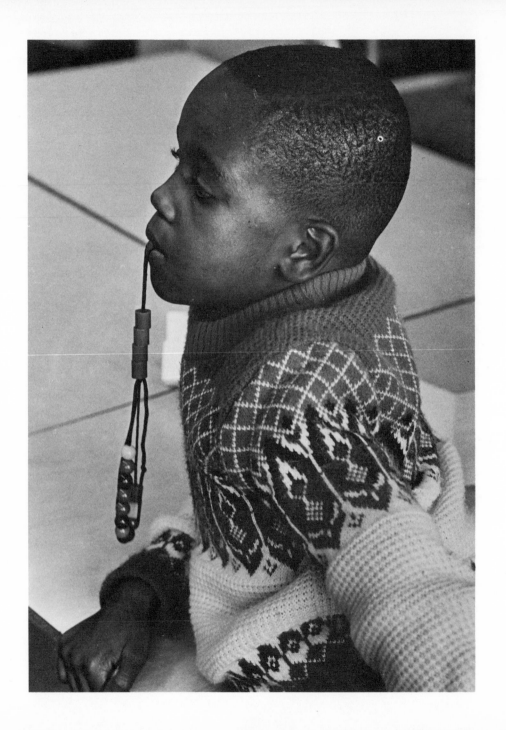

Vernon

How can you describe a little five-year-old boy who begs to be killed, who wants passionately to die because living is so difficult for him?

Five years old and about thirty inches high. He is a miniature—tiny feet, hands, short legs. How they find him clothes I do not know; they buy him shoes with fairly high heels (the kind hipsters wear).

He has a strange, quiet face; he never talked, just stared with large eyes. And did exactly as he pleased, no matter what the group did, no matter what the class rules. Punishment had no effect; deprivation of privileges did not seem to penetrate. Stubbornness such as cannot be believed—like granite; as though he were rooted to the very center of the earth.

This is going to sound prejudiced—his face is what I would draw for one of the Imps of Hell. He looks like a bastion of the Devil (don't I sound medieval?), and he behaves accordingly.

It was incredible that such a little one would seek punishment so avidly. It had to be that, because he so flagrantly did not do what he knew very well he should.

Talk about self-image, my God! How this child sees himself! How could I reach him? So I started to praise him for whatever I could—new shirt, new suspenders, haircut, anything—and with it I always managed to pet him physically (I refused to dislike him, much as he tried to make me). Finally he broke out in a wide grin, and it was like turning on the sun. He became all smile and light and started to cooperate a bit. I never missed an opportunity to praise him and show that I cared about what he did.

The upshot was that he finally began to talk. I discovered he could speak very well, articulately and interestingly, and we became friends.

Then he was absent for a few days. When he came back his face was covered with bruises. When questioned he finally revealed the fact that his father had beaten him about the face as he sat on the sofa, "for nothin'!" Knowing Vernon as I do, he could provoke a saint. Given a drink or two, and being egged on by Vernon (who has developed quite a skillful technique for irritating an adult), his father must have lashed out. The next time he will kill the boy—and fulfill the boy's deepest wish. I hope to God we may avert any more punishment for the child.

But the beating sent Vernon back into being the quiet, stubborn little iconoclast.

A dollar's worth of gas

In the morning Mr. Downer and I took lower-primary-grade boys to the tire company and the gas station. When we came back, the teacher asked some questions concerning the trip. Among them he asked, "What would you say when you need gasoline at the station?" No answer. The teacher continued, "Probably you would say, 'Fill it up.'" Suddenly strong disagreement came from one of the boys. He said, "No, you would say, 'Give me a dollar's worth of gas.'"

"I Cuban! I speak Spanish!"

Rafael's family fled from Cuba. The family had been very wealthy but now were starting from scratch here in America.

Rafael spoke no English but soon learned to understand. He was a smart boy and after a few months began to try to outsmart me. Whenever he chose not to obey me, he would pretend he did not understand. He spoke English with his peers and had no trouble understanding them. In fact, I discovered he was teaching his parents how to speak English. After a particularly trying day, I made some comment to him about his use of English. "I no learn English! I Cuban! I speak Spanish!"

I wonder if this isn't the same feeling some of our central-city children have regarding their teachers.

Staff meeting today

A half-day off so teachers can discuss issues crucial to the school, and what gets discussed?—the condition of the furniture in the teacher's room!! Honest! Then we went on to the dirty floors and broken chairs in the auditorium! Always the symptoms, never the causes.

How can a group of grownups of supposed intelligence avoid the issues at hand? What is it that makes everyone, including myself, keep his mouth shut? There were many who were aching to really discuss the issues.

My answers are: (1) The inability or unwillingness of the principal to lead the discussion in that direction. I think this man, though competent in many areas, is afraid to attack issues in a roomful of forty-five teachers. (2) His fear probably comes from the nature of our staff. It is unfortunately split. The Negro teachers (about twenty) are extremely vocal and extremely close-minded. *They* brought up and discussed the teachers' room. They segregate themselves in the room, and believe it or not, every day they take their lunches to a teacher's room rather than eating in the teachers' lunchroom. They like strict discipline and have no time or patience for problems. It's the teacher's fault—she can whip her kids into shape and avoid problems if she wants, and so cleanliness in the teacher's room becomes the only issue left. Am I generalizing, oversimplifying, or being prejudiced? No. It's a condition all teachers in our school will admit exists.

What can I do to stop it? I wish I knew—I'm scared stiff when this group is together and I have to interrupt for something. They are a terribly vain and superior group—and I am a lowly white teacher vainly attempting to handle "their" kids. Believe me, I feel only sadness and frustration that I am powerless.

A matter of policy

I was confused. He was telling me that I couldn't take the children on a field trip to see how the department stores prepare for Christmas. Why? I didn't understand. Isn't taking trips part of good teaching? I heard phrases like "a great distance," "Are they ready?" "Keep track of them." These could be reasons for not going, but not effective reasons. Still confused.

As I backed out of the principal's office, thanking him (why do we thank people for saying no to us?), his real reason finally came out—

"You know that shoplifting is such a problem with this type of child."

The friendly policeman

I went to the zoo with a third-grade class. The teacher divided the class, so I led half of them, and as we were walking a policeman drove by. I stopped him, and the children all clustered around. He talked kindly to them, then said to me, when he saw the one white child, "She must be here by mistake."

After all, they ARE people

We had a demonstration with our micro class. The children in the experiment got into a discussion on racial discrimination. Poor Kevin sat surrounded by white classmates and white teacher and white observers. After the experiment the greatest reaction among observers was of Kevin's lack of participation in the discussion. After all, we are their friends, we are trying to help them sort of react. The discussion of the children had simply bristled with sage observations, "After all, they *are* people!" What a noble concession! After an overture of friendship and understanding like that, how crude of Kevin not to respond. This is the hope of the future, Kevin. No doubt you've met similar situations before. No doubt at all you'll meet them again. Hang on, Kevin, life is chuck full of ignorance.

Three colored men in a boat

One of my children told me the joke about the three colored men in a boat, named Do, Re, guess the third, Mi. I could hear her telling this to her mixed audience and panicked. What to say and how to react? Now she was telling me, and I could no longer avoid the issue. "What's so funny, Mary?" I didn't want to underreact or overreact. Inside I was angry and indignant at such stupidity and cruelty in a joke. What did my black students think of a joke whose humor depended on the victim being tricked into saying he was colored, and then being laughed at for his "foolishness"? And who will tell me how to handle such a situation? Were I alone with the girl, she would have made this her last racial joke. But to prolong an embarrassing situation for those victimized did not seem the right thing to do.

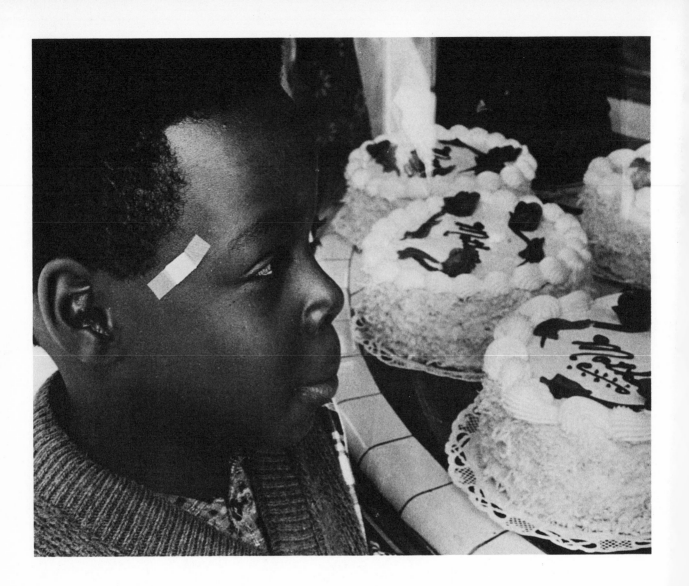

Chin Chin Chinaman!

"Chin Chin Chinaman!" It was one of my students screaming this at an Oriental boy of another grade. "You apologize!" I heard myself ordering. Egad, just like a teacher. Exactly like one! I felt ridiculous, but it was too late. "Apologize!" I said again. "I'm sorry," replied Michael, but the other little boy had wandered off somewhere. So that meaningless little episode over, we marched back into the classroom where all was forgotten except the stupidity of my demand for an apology, which lingered on in my peewee brain and will stay there long enough, I hope, to prevent the same occurrence in the future.

Summer in Milwaukee

This summer, driving from home to the University daily, I tried to take various routes through the inner-city area. On hot, humid, "godawful" days, I examined the crowded porches and door stoops and noticed the cracked and crumbling curbing, the number of doorways with no screen doors, the broken windows, peeling paint, etc., etc. The smell of beer drifted from bars from which the sound of whirring fans was audible. Children were playing on the unsmooth strips of sidewalk before the houses and in front of the stores and taverns. I have, since moving to Milwaukee seven months ago, tried to analyze my feelings and attitudes about the Negro. I think that if I lived with five or six people in a small two-bedroom bungalow sandwiched between other similar houses (allowing little or no cross ventilation) *and* the temperature was 93 degrees, humidity 95 per cent, *and* I was sitting on a very dilapidated, crowded porch in the evening wishing I could afford to buy a six-pack of beer, *and* a woman like myself came riding slowly by in a half-paid-for VW— I might very easily be driven to do something unlawful or outrageous—like tipping the VW upside down or asking the woman what in the hell she's doing snooping around the neighborhood.

I took my self-indulgent sister-in-law to the neighborhood near Eighth Street School yesterday and listened to her comments. (Incidentally, she is also from LaCrosse and believes she is enlightened on the racial situation in the United States because she went to high school with one Negro boy.)

Phrases used in social welfare

1. Undifferentiated ego mass (family).
2. "The first tool we use in social work is ourselves."
3. Psychic interaction.
4. The ultimate group.
5. "The group is a terrific laboratory."
6. Structured relationships.

Blockbusting

"You know, in our sociology course this last semester, the professor said that it's been proven: one Negro family moves into an all-white neighborhood, runs down the house, the other neighbors move out, the Negroes move in, and then a slum has been created." Observing the Negro neighborhood in Milwaukee, she said that maybe it was a good thing they were "with their kind."

I explained to her, while driving by the school I will be teaching in this fall, that there were many factors involved—absentee landlords, "the culture of poverty," de facto segregation . . . She remained inflexible in her thinking. I listen to and observe her reactions and realize that this was me five or six years ago.

They have rhythm in their bones . . .

It was a coffee break during our music workshop at the school board. The instructor gave a shifty glance toward Cynthia and with a mouthy whisper informed me quite confidentially that *they* had rhythm in their bones and I should capitalize on this in my teaching. Let me introduce Cynthia. Cynthia is the one reason we call our class of ten integrated. Did you notice the perfect proportion? Exactly 10 per cent black— we can speak of Eastern Europeans being especially adept at folk dances, or speak of the Irish tenor or the famous Italian opera stars, but to say the Negro is particularly adept at rhythmical skills is somehow thought to be derogatory. That is because the whole area of relationships between any ethnic group and Negroes has become, over the years, strained to the point of extreme sensitivity, like a badly infected and swollen knee. We find it easiest to deal with obvious differences by pretending that none exist, when it is really quite evident that, accentuated by segregational social customs, there are definite cultural differences between Negroes and the other groups. We can learn from these and profit, too, if we but recognize them and take the time to study them.

Money?

Who has money?
Do you?
Who has money?
Does he?
Who has money?
Does she?
Who needs money?
ME!

Grace

"You're the most stupid bitch I've ever met, Grace.
You really are. You think I was after Flora. You're
wrong, Grace." Whack and a moan. "I wasn't after
her, I wanted that bag's daughter, you hear, Grace,
I was after her daughter."

Several sobs could be heard across the court.
A prostitute cried and listened to the terrible truth.
A man let all the world hear the terrible truth.

"Grace, you got no right to talk about Flora.
You're not my wife. My wife wouldn't talk like you."
Another slap. Grace sobbed long, low sobs.

"You ain't my wife, Grace. I ain't never goin' to
fuck you again, Grace. Now I'll tell you somethin'.
You get the hell out of here, Grace. Take that little
bastard with you. You is stupid, Grace, the most
stupid woman I ever met. You hear Grace?"

Neither Grace nor the man left that night, but the
sobs continued from time to time.

Epilogue

Tonight Grace and the same man are together.

125

Strip

"The Detention Home is not a penal institution. A boy or girl is held until he or she is bound over for trial or sentenced to a correctional institution. It is like a home away from home." That's what we were told.

In the Home there is maximum security.

The Home runs like this. A child is led into a room where he or she is stripped and showered. The child is under surveillance all the time. Clothes are issued. The child lives in a cell locked tight. All rooms are locked.

Someone else's business is not mine

Sunday morning at 3 a.m. I heard a series of blood-curdling screams from some woman. "He's killing me, he's killing me," and screams which sounded as though someone was being murdered.

I ran to the window but saw no scuffle. A man was walking his dog, and continued, apparently not intending to take any part. Another man walked by, also disregarding anything.

Then the screams stopped. I had decided there was nothing I could do if these men, bigger and stronger than I, were not going to offer any help, and I stayed upstairs.

Later, I learned that G——— had come down and was told to stay out of it, that what happened at the other hotel was not to be interfered with by anyone in this hotel, and vice versa.

A man had been trying to take a girl to a hotel, and apparently beat her up when she refused to go in. The "law" came, and we learned nothing further, but I'll never forget the screams.

The judge

Justice has been defined as "rendering to every man what is due to him." Pascal believed justice to be definable in the abstract but unobtainable in the concrete.

Everyone is entitled to legal counsel. Some men, on occasion, choose to defend themselves in a court; others have no choice but to defend themselves because they can't afford or do not trust a lawyer.

Yesterday, in about seven minutes, a boy about nineteen was sentenced to ninety days in the House of Correction. The judge in his chamber spoke of the rapidity with which he disposes of such cases. He rendered swift justice.

The lady walked quickly away

As I was waiting for the "Don't Walk" to change, licking my strawberry ice cream cone, a voice behind me—unseen, then seen—asked, "May I have a lick of your ice cream cone?" I handed it to her. While she was licking I noted her bright, attractive orange dress against her brown skin and her age (late twenties probably). I waited for her to return the cone to me because germs aren't an aversion, but when she continued to lick I smiled and said that if she wished, she could have it, "because calorie-wise it wasn't so good for me." She then stepped behind me and mashed the cone with the remaining ice cream in it down the back of my dress. The lady walked quickly away—on the curb, then off. I stood and watched her for a while, then waited for the "Walk" light and went home.

Universities are the sand..

All I keep seeing is Russia of the 1920's, when chaos ruled and gangs of children wandered around plundering. It seems to me we are heading that way, that the sand for all ostriches to hide in is our own universities where research is going on, oblivious to anything outside the ivy halls. Ruin is on its way.

Baptism under fire

And now I've had it—baptism under fire. Today Elvin decided to lie prone on the floor when the rest were sitting down to listen to a story. I asked him twice to get up. When there was no response, I dragged him into the coatroom and told him to stay there until he decided to sit with others.

Whereupon I unleashed all the Furies and their relatives! His anger and fury—it went beyond anger and fury and frustration—it went into a form of insanity—violent insanity.

First, he threw around all the boots in the room. Then he pulled a coat down and lashed it around a table, pulling at it as though he would strangle the table. He used vehement language. None of this got a rise out of me. He quieted down, waiting for me to come. When I did, he threw himself against the wall in a corner and looked as though he'd tear down the wall. He wears glasses fastened to his head with an elastic headband. He had removed this protective band, and I was concerned that he would break the glasses and hurt himself. I managed to get hold of the glasses intact, which infuriated him further. I left him at that point, having put his glasses safely high up.

But he was not finished.

He looked hysterically around to see what else would provide ammunition for this uncontrollable hysteria. He caught sight of a box of wood that we use for teaching woodworking. He started to take everything out of it, and since the box was as tall as he, he got deeper into it. I came along and helped him by trying to push him in. Although this seemed to have been his original intent, he did not welcome my help.

Unbeknownst to me, much of this was being observed by the principal, vice-principal, cooperating teacher, and the social worker who was handling Elvin's family case.

Here the vice-principal stepped in and pulled him out, and I caught glimpses of him being held by a man teacher. He was screaming and straining and punching and pummeling. Elvin is five years old!

He was sent up to the counselor. By the time he got there the fit was over, and the counselor had a sweet little boy to handle. Elvin got what he wanted —the sole attention of an adult.

The children all recognized the sick behavior. They did not side with him and were horrified by the violent reactions.

Elvin is the brother of the notorious Sam, who gives each teacher hell in her classroom, and behaves like a model child for psychiatrists, who do not recommend treatment.

In discussing this later I learned that Elvin was deathly afraid of fire. Previous to his behavior we had had a bomb alert drill.

By the principal's office

There was Rhonda, out in the hall by the principal's office. What was she doing there? She didn't want to go to gym with the class.

So I asked her if she would help me clean the paint cans in the kindergarten. She seemed happy to, and while she was helping me I asked her why she had refused to go. "I got no pants on." "Then why didn't you tell your teacher?" "He's a man." Then, "Mrs. Roth, I wouldn't have gone if I had pants on." "Why not?" "Because he hit me with a ruler."

Sincerely,

Relationships with children at school are no effort, but trying to establish a professional atmosphere with my principal became impossible.

Seldom did he appear in my classroom (like twice during one school year), but when "Doc" wanted to talk over something, be it urgent or trivia, in walked a sixth-grade monitor, folded note in hand. The notes were usually to the point.

```
Office,
        R.
```

The only response was to appear in the office immediately. It really didn't matter if the children were very involved in a reading or thinking experience, I was to get my ass down to the office. No response on my part usually brought a second note written with greater impatience.

```
Waiting,
         R.
```

One time I received a note about 10:45 a.m. with his favorite inscription, "Office—R." A reading group was very involved with their work and needed my presence. I ran to the office giving the children the excuse that the principal had something important to discuss with me. He got me into his office and told me that my hair was too long. "Get a haircut. You look like Herman from *Herman's Hermits!* The children will not respect you with your hair like that."

Eventually I dealt with the problem as professionally as I could: whenever a note came and I felt I couldn't leave, I responded by giving the monitor a note in return.

```
As soon as possible.
                   H.
```

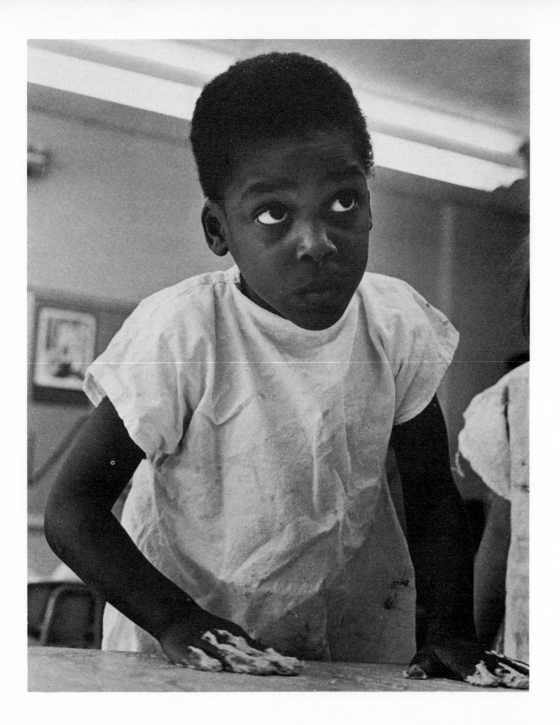

Ada

Ada rises every morning and dresses herself to come to school. Her mother has five children to care for. Two have visual handicaps and require the most attention. On the last day of summer school, I walked to the car, loaded with tomato plants, styrofoam sticks, and what not. Ada met me at the car to say goodbye. I told her that she could have a tomato plant if her mother would consent. Mrs. V. came to the door of their home, invited me to the porch. We talked about raising tomato plants but went on to discuss Ada's progress in school this summer.

I am an activist:
some daydreams about teaching

I turn from the blackboard to face the class as the tall Negro youth rises in the back row. He has a handkerchief over his hand because someone has told him that gunmen silence their weapons with handkerchiefs.

I am not calm, but my voice is dispassionate. "Did you make the gun yourself?" I ask. He is silent.

"I said did you make the gun yourself? Or"—I pause, throwing a piece of chalk in the air and catching it easily—"did your father help you?"

The class gasps and the boy tightens his grasp on his gun. The handkerchief partially falls away and I can see that it is a .38 automatic Wesson, for I was a naval hero. "My father," the boy says.

"You know," I interrupt, "you don't have to shoot me for me to like you . . ."

Sociological generalizations

"Within this culture of poverty it is perfectly all right to take things from the out-group as long as you never take from the in-group."—*Bruno Bettelheim*

"A few weeks ago I sent Diane to cash a check. This man gave her the money and the check, too. I kept the check for a few days and then cashed it again. It was $98, too. Stupid man!"—*Lana*

The lemon choir bus

As a carhop for one summer in my cousin's root beer stand, I was fascinated with the faces of the Negroes, most of them workingmen, who lined the counter each noon hour. I remember noting their hair and the perspiration on their faces and thinking over and over again that this was the first time I had really *seen* a Negro or talked to him. One very warm Sunday evening around eleven o'clock, my thirteen-year-old cousin and I boarded the Lemon Choir bus to take the orders from the Negro men, women, and children who looked exhausted and uncomfortable in the dim light of the stuffy interior. Later both Myra and I discussed the incident with other young people working with us and with my married cousins with whom we were staying. I heard references made to "the smelly niggers," "coons," "those black boys," "their nigger lips." The question we were most often asked: "Were you scared?" I know that at the time I was apprehensive about confronting so many Negroes at one time, and later when we were all laughing about the incident I felt as if I had accomplished some great feat by entering the bus.

Negro history week

I do not know why we have Negro history week. Maybe because white people want it. All I know it is Negro history week.   *Jimmie*

Individualizing instruction

"This is too hard! Don't you have any cutting or pasting for me to do?"

(*Third Grade*)

They

They, they, they—wherever I go, white people refer
to Negroes as THEY. When anyone learns that I
teach in a black school, the remarks are:

"THEY're cute when THEY're little, aren't they?"

"I guess THEY should have open housing, but I
wouldn't want THEM living near me."

Not the time to begin

The counselor is in the old North annex.
A tired light on the ceiling burns
while the two of them remain silent,
the counselor . . .
and the kid
who
has just driven his fist, like a blunt
steel plug at the end of a thick
drive shaft
into the center of an English teacher's
face.

The counselor
does not think
that it is the time to begin . . .
He does not know
when the time will be.
An old radiator—cast iron
and dirty silver—
trickles to
itself.

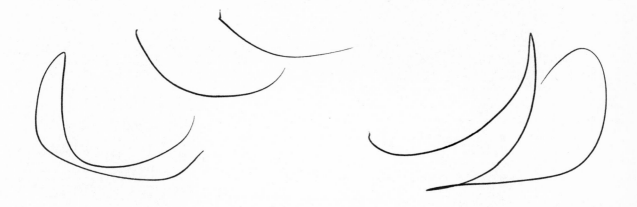